THE JU

In the hills of Southern India a baby lies warm and safe in a cave. He lies among wolf-cubs, next to Mother Wolf's side, and he is not afraid. Outside the cave Shere Khan, the man-eating tiger, roars angrily, wanting to kill. 'No!' says Mother Wolf. 'The man's cub belongs to me. He will live, to run with the other wolves, to be my son. And I will call him Mowgli.'

The years pass, and Mowgli the man's cub grows up with the wolves. He learns the Law of the Jungle from his teachers, Baloo the old brown bear and Bagheera the black panther. He has many adventures, and many friends among the animals of the jungle.

But he still has an enemy. Shere Khan the tiger has not forgotten. He waits for the day when he can catch the man's cub – and kill him.

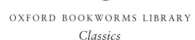

OXFORD BOOKWORMS LIBRARY

Classics

The Jungle Book

Stage 2 (700 headwords)

Series Editor: Jennifer Bassett
Founder Editor: Tricia Hedge
Activities Editors: Jennifer Bassett and Alison Baxter

RUDYARD KIPLING

The Jungle Book

Retold by
Ralph Mowat

Illustrated by
Kanako Damerum and Yuzuru Takasaki

OXFORD UNIVERSITY PRESS

OXFORD

UNIVERSITY PRESS

Great Clarendon Street, Oxford OX2 6DP

Oxford University Press is a department of the University of Oxford.
It furthers the University's objective of excellence in research, scholarship,
and education by publishing worldwide in

Oxford New York

Auckland Cape Town Dar es Salaam Hong Kong Karachi
Kuala Lumpur Madrid Melbourne Mexico City Nairobi
New Delhi Shanghai Taipei Toronto

With offices in

Argentina Austria Brazil Chile Czech Republic France Greece
Guatemala Hungary Italy Japan Poland Portugal Singapore
South Korea Switzerland Thailand Turkey Ukraine Vietnam

OXFORD and OXFORD ENGLISH are registered trade marks of
Oxford University Press in the UK and in certain other countries

This simplified edition © Oxford University Press 2008

Database right Oxford University Press (maker)

First published in Oxford Bookworms 1997

6 8 10 9 7

ISBN 978 0 19 479064 2

A complete recording of this Bookworms edition of
The Jungle Book is available on audio CD ISBN 978 0 19 478987 5

Printed in China

ACKNOWLEDGEMENTS
Illustrated by: Kanako & Yuzuru at Thorogood.net

Word count (main text): 6510 words

For more information on the Oxford Bookworms Library,
visit www.oup.com/bookworms

CONTENTS

Mowgli's brothers

One very warm evening in the Seeonee hills in Southern India, Father Wolf woke up from his day's rest. Next to him lay Mother Wolf, with their four cubs beside her.

'It's time to look for food,' said Father Wolf, and he stood up to leave the cave.

'Good luck,' said a voice. It was the jackal, Tabaqui, who eats everything and anything, even pieces of old clothes from the villages. The wolves of India do not like him, because he runs around making trouble and telling bad stories about them.

'Shere Khan, the tiger, is coming to look for food here,' said Tabaqui.

'Shere Khan is coming to look for food.'

'He can't,' cried Father Wolf. 'By the Law of the Jungle he must tell us first, *before* he comes here to hunt.'

'Shere Khan has a bad leg, so he can kill only cows. In the village near him the people are angry. That is why he is coming here – to start hunting in a new place. Listen, you can hear him now,' said Tabaqui.

'He is a stupid animal,' said Father Wolf, and he listened to the angry noise of a tiger who has not eaten. 'No one will find anything to eat in the jungle now.'

'But Shere Khan is hunting man, not animal, tonight,' said Tabaqui.

The Law of the Jungle says that animals must not hunt man, because man-killing brings men with guns. Then everybody in the jungle is in danger.

Father and Mother Wolf listened to Shere Khan in the jungle not far away. Then, suddenly, they heard a noise much nearer to them.

'It's a man. A man's cub. Look!' said Father Wolf.

And there in front of them stood a baby who could just walk. He looked up at Father Wolf and laughed.

'Is that a man's cub?' asked Mother Wolf. 'I have never seen one. Bring it here.'

The baby, small and with no clothes, pushed its way between the cubs to get near to Mother Wolf. 'Look,' she said, 'he is taking his meal with the others.'

'I have heard that this has happened before,' said

'It's a man. A man's cub. Look!' said Father Wolf.

Father Wolf, 'but I have never seen it until now. Look at him. He is not afraid.'

Suddenly, it was dark, and Shere Khan was pushing his great head in through the mouth of the cave.

'We are pleased that you visit us, Shere Khan,' said Father Wolf, but his eyes were angry. 'What do you need?'

'I am hunting a man's cub,' said Shere Khan. 'Its father and mother have run away. Give it to me.'

Father Wolf knew that Shere Khan could not get inside the cave because he was too big.

'The man's cub belongs to us,' he said. 'The Pack – the other wolves and I – will decide. If we want to kill him, *we* will kill him, not you.'

'The man's cub belongs to me! It is I, Shere Khan, who speaks!' And Shere Khan's roar filled the cave with noise.

'No!' came the angry voice of Mother Wolf. 'The man's cub belongs to me! We will not kill him. He will live, to run with the other wolves, to be my son. Now go away, fish-killer, eater of cubs! Go!'

Shere Khan went. He knew that he could not fight Mother Wolf in the cave. 'But I will have this man-cub one day, you thieves!' he shouted from the jungle.

'Do you really want to keep him, Mother?' said Father Wolf.

'Keep him?' said Mother Wolf. 'Yes. He came here by night, alone and hungry, but he was not afraid. Yes,

I will keep him. And I will call him Mowgli, the frog.'

'But what will the other wolves of the Pack say?'

By the Law of the Jungle all wolf-cubs must come to the Pack when they can walk. The wolves look at the cubs carefully.

'Mowgli, the frog'

Then the cubs are free to run anywhere because all the adult wolves know them and will not attack them.

When the four wolf-cubs could run a little, Father Wolf took them and Mowgli and Mother Wolf to the Meeting Rock. Here, the hundred wolves of the Wolf-Pack met every month when the moon was full.

The leader of the Pack was Akela, a great grey wolf. Each new wolf-cub came to stand in front of him and Akela said, 'Look well, O Wolves. Look well!'

At the end, Father Wolf pushed Mowgli into the circle of wolves. Then from the trees outside the circle they heard the voice of Shere Khan.

'The man-cub belongs to me. Give him to me!'

Akela did not move but said only, 'Look well! Who speaks for this man-cub? Two voices, who are not his father and mother, must speak for him.'

There is only one other animal who can come to these wolf-meetings – Baloo, the sleepy brown bear. His job is to teach the Law of the Jungle to the wolf-cubs.

'I speak for the man-cub,' came Baloo's deep voice. 'Let him run with the Pack. I myself will teach him.'

'We need another voice to speak for him,' said Akela.

Silently, another animal jumped down into the circle. It was Bagheera the panther, black as the night, clever, strong, and dangerous.

'O Akela, will you let me speak?' said Bagheera softly. 'The Law of the Jungle says it is possible to buy the life of a cub. It is bad to kill a man-cub. He cannot hurt you. Let him live with you, and I will give you a fat cow, newly killed, which lies in the jungle not far away.'

The voices of the wolves replied, 'Let him live.' They were always hungry and they wanted to get the dead cow. Soon they went away, and there were only Akela, Bagheera, Baloo, and Mowgli's wolf family left. They could hear the angry roars of Shere Khan in the night.

'It is good,' said Akela. 'Men are clever. Perhaps this man-cub will help us when he is older. Take him away,'

'O Akela, will you let me speak?' said Bagheera softly.

he said to Father Wolf, 'and teach him well. '

And so, because of Baloo's good word and the present of a cow, Mowgli now belonged to the Seeonee Wolf-Pack.

~~~

The story of Mowgli's life among the wolves fills many books, but we must jump ten or eleven years now. Father Wolf, Baloo, and Bagheera taught Mowgli well, and he learnt everything about the jungle. He knew the meaning of every sound in the trees, of every song of the birds, of every splash in the water. He learnt to climb trees like a monkey, to swim in the rivers like a fish, and to hunt for his food as cleverly as any animal in the jungle.

2
The Monkey-People

Baloo, the old brown bear, loved teaching Mowgli. He taught him how to speak to the different Jungle-People, and he taught him the important Master-Words. But Mowgli sometimes got bored with all the lessons. One day, when he was not listening, Baloo hit him, very softly, on the head, and Mowgli ran away angrily.

Bagheera, the black panther, was not happy about this. 'Remember how small he is,' he said to Baloo. 'How can his little head hold all your long words?'

'These words will keep him safe from the birds, from

the Snake-People, and all the animals that hunt,' said Baloo. 'It is true that he is only small. But no one will hurt him, if he remembers all the Master-Words. Come, Mowgli!' he called into the trees. 'Come and say the words again.'

Mowgli climbed down from a tree and came to sit next to them. 'I will say the words to Bagheera, not *you*, fat old Baloo!' he said crossly.

'Very well,' said Baloo sadly. 'Say the words for the Hunting-People.'

'We are of one blood, you and I,' said Mowgli.

'Good. Now for the birds.'

Mowgli climbed down from a tree.

Mowgli said the same words but with the sound of a bird.

'Now for the Snake-People,' said Baloo.

Mowgli then made the long 'ssss' sound, which was like no other noise, only the noise of a snake.

'Good,' said Baloo gently. 'One day you will thank me for my lessons. Now you will be safe in the jungle, because no snake, no bird, no animal will hurt you. You do not need to be afraid of anyone.'

'And I shall have my people and go with them high up in the trees,' shouted Mowgli.

'What did you say, Mowgli?' asked Baloo, surprised. 'Have you been with the *Bandar-log*, the Monkey-People?'

Mowgli could hear that Baloo was angry, and he saw too that Bagheera's green eyes were cold and hard.

'When Baloo hurt my head,' said Mowgli, 'I went away, and the grey monkeys came down from the trees and talked to me. They were kind to me and gave me nice things to eat. Then they took me up into the trees. They said that I was their brother, and they wanted me to be their leader one day. Why have you never told me about the Monkey-People? Bad old Baloo! They play all day and don't do lessons, and I will play with them again.'

'Listen, man-cub,' said Baloo angrily. 'I have taught you the Law for all the Jungle-People, but not for the Monkey-People. They have no law. Their ways are not our ways. They are noisy and dirty, and they think that they are a great people, but then they forget everything. The rest of the Jungle-People do not talk to them, or even think about them. Remember what I tell you.'

Mowgli listened, and was sorry. But all this time the *Bandar-log* were above them in the trees, listening and watching. They followed Mowgli and his friends through the jungle until it was time for the midday rest. Mowgli lay between his friends and went to sleep,

But all this time the Bandar-log *were listening and watching.*

11

saying, 'I will never talk to or play with the Monkey-People again.'

When he woke up, he was high in a tree and there were hands holding his legs and arms – hard, strong, little hands. Down below Baloo was shouting angrily, and Bagheera was trying to climb up the tree, but he was too heavy for the thin branches. The monkeys, shouting and laughing, carried Mowgli between them and began their journey along the monkey roads, which are high in the trees.

It was a wild, exciting journey. The monkeys jumped from tree-top to tree-top, crashing through the leaves and branches. At first Mowgli was afraid of falling, but then he began to think. He must tell Baloo and Bagheera where he was. High up in the blue sky he saw Chil the kite. The big bird saw that the monkeys were carrying a man-cub. He flew down to look, and was surprised to hear the bird-call of the kites: 'We are of one blood, you and I!'

'Who are you?' called Chil.

'Mowgli, the man-cub!' came the reply. 'Watch where they take me, and tell Baloo and Bagheera.'

'I will,' called Chil, and he flew high above the trees and watched with his far-seeing eyes.

Monkeys can travel fast when they want to, and by now Baloo and Bagheera were a long way behind.

Chil the kite flew down to look.

'We cannot follow the *Bandar-log* through the trees,' said Baloo, 'and we will never catch them. But they are afraid of Kaa, the big python. He can climb as easily as the monkeys, and he eats them. Perhaps he will help us.' And so Baloo and Bagheera went to look for Kaa the python.

They found him, lying in the sun – ten metres of brown-and-yellow snake, beautiful and dangerous.

'What news?' called Kaa when he saw them.

'We are looking for food,' said Baloo. He knew that you must not hurry Kaa. He is too big.

'Let me come with you,' said Kaa hungrily. 'I have not eaten for days.'

13

'We are following the *Bandar-log*,' said Baloo. 'Those noisy, dirty thieves have stolen our man-cub. And we love our man-cub very much, Kaa!'

'The *Bandar-log*,' said Bagheera cleverly, 'are very much afraid of you, Kaa. But they say bad things about you, and call you "old yellow fish", I hear.'

'Tss! Tss!' said Kaa. 'I will teach them not to call me bad names. Where did they take your man-cub? They will be tired of him quickly, and that is bad for him.'

'Up! Up! Look up, Baloo!'

Baloo looked up and saw Chil the kite, high in the sky.

'What is it?' called Baloo.

'I will teach them not to call me bad names,' said Kaa.

'I have seen Mowgli the man-cub with the *Bandar-log*. He knew the Master-Word. They have taken him to the monkey-city, the Lost City.'

Baloo and Bagheera knew of the monkey-city. Men lived there once, but they left hundreds of years ago. Nobody went there now, only the *Bandar-log*.

'We must leave at once,' said Bagheera. 'It is a long way.'

'I will come as fast as I can,' said Baloo, 'but you and Kaa can go faster. I will follow you.'

The Lost City was very old. There were many beautiful buildings, but the walls were broken and full of holes, and there were tall trees in houses that were now open to the sky. The Monkey-People called the place their city, and ran around everywhere, in and out of the empty houses, up and down the fruit trees in the old gardens.

Now Mowgli was in their city, and the Monkey-People were very pleased with themselves. 'This boy can help us,' they said. 'He can teach us how to make things, because men are clever with their hands.' But monkeys make many plans, and always forget them five minutes later.

When Mowgli arrived in the city, he was tired and hungry. 'Bring me food,' he said, and twenty or thirty monkeys ran to bring him fruit. But they started fighting and forgot to take any fruit back to Mowgli.

Mowgli knew that he was in a bad place. 'Baloo was

The Monkey-People called the place their city.

right,' he thought. 'The *Bandar-log* have no Law and their ways are not our ways. I must try to get away. Baloo will surely be angry with me, but that is better than life with the *Bandar-log*.'

But when Mowgli went to the walls of the city, the

monkeys pulled him back. 'You are very happy here with us. We are great. We are wonderful. We all say so, and so it is true,' they shouted.

'Don't they ever sleep?' thought Mowgli. He looked up at the sky. 'There's a cloud coming over the moon. Perhaps I can run away when it's dark. But I am tired.'

Kaa's hunting

Bagheera and Kaa were also watching that cloud. They were now outside the city walls, but they knew they had to be careful. There were only two of them, and there were hundreds of monkeys.

'They are over there by that house, talking about the boy,' said Bagheera. 'When the cloud hides the moon, I will attack them.'

'I will go to the higher ground at the west wall,' Kaa said, 'and come down the hill very fast. Good hunting!'

The black panther ran quickly to the crowds of monkeys and started hitting, right and left, as hard as he could. The monkeys screamed angrily, but then one of them shouted, 'There is only one here! Kill him! Kill!' And a crowd of monkeys jumped on Bagheera, biting and pulling. Another group pulled Mowgli up a wall and pushed him over. He fell down into a dark room which had no doors or windows, and he could not get out. 'Stay there,' shouted the monkeys, 'until we have killed your friend. And then we will play with you, if the snakes leave you alive.'

Mowgli heard hissing sounds in the darkness around him. 'We are of one blood, you and I,' he said, quickly giving the Snakes' Call.

'Sssss,' the snakes replied. 'We will not bite you, but stand still, Little Brother, because your feet can hurt us.'

Mowgli stood very still and listened to the fight around Bagheera. For the first time ever, the big panther was fighting for his life. Then Mowgli remembered something. There was a big tank of water near one of the buildings.

'Go to the tank, Bagheera! Get to the water!'

Bagheera heard and he knew that Mowgli was safe. Suddenly he felt stronger and he pulled himself slowly to the tank, fighting against the crowds of monkeys.

Then Baloo came running in from the jungle, shouting, 'Bagheera, I am here!' At once the monkeys jumped on him, and the bear started to hit them with his great strong arms. Mowgli heard a splash when Bagheera jumped into the tank. The monkeys were afraid of water and could not follow him there. But they stood all round the sides, ready to jump on him if he tried to get out and help Baloo.

And where was Kaa all this time? It was a hard climb up to the west wall, and Kaa moved carefully over the stones. Now he came down the hill very quickly, hungry and wanting to kill. Kaa was ten metres long, heavy and strong. He went silently into the crowd of monkeys around Baloo, and he did not need to hit twice.

When they are very young, monkeys are told about Kaa, the silent thief who can kill the strongest monkey.

Mowgli heard a splash when Bagheera jumped into the tank.

19

All monkeys are afraid of Kaa. Now they ran, with shouts of 'It's Kaa! Run! Run!'

Then Kaa opened his mouth for the first time and spoke one long hissing word. The monkeys were suddenly silent and still, and nothing moved in the city.

Bagheera pulled himself out of the tank. 'Get the man-cub out and let us go,' he said. 'I can't fight any more. And the monkeys will attack us again.'

'It's Kaa! Run! Run!'

'They will not move until I tell them to move,' said Kaa.

'We must thank you, Kaa. We could not do it without you,' said Baloo.

'I am happy to help. Where is the man-cub?' said Kaa.

'Here! In this room, but I cannot get out.'

'Take him away,' called the snakes around Mowgli. 'He dances around too much and he will stand on us.'

'Stand back, man-cub,' said Kaa. 'I will break the wall.'

With two metres of his heavy body off the ground, Kaa hit the wall very hard, five or six times. A hole opened, and Mowgli jumped quickly through it. He ran and put his arms around Baloo and Bagheera.

'Are you hurt?' asked Baloo.

'Not much,' said Mowgli, 'but the *Bandar-log* have hurt you badly, my friends.'

'It is nothing,' said Baloo. 'But you must thank Kaa. He has done much for you tonight.'

Mowgli turned and saw the head of the great python.

'So this is the man-cub,' said Kaa. 'He is like the *Bandar-log*, but not the same. Be careful, man-cub, that I do not make a mistake when I am hunting monkeys.'

'We are of one blood, you and I,' Mowgli answered. 'You have given me my life tonight. When I kill, it will be for you if you are hungry.'

'Well spoken,' said Baloo.

'You are brave, young man,' said Kaa, 'and you speak

well. Now go with your friends. The moon is going down. You must not see what will happen here next.'

Kaa went softly out in front of the lines of sitting monkeys and began to dance. His head moved from right to left, and his long body turned this way and that way, making circles that changed every second. Slowly, never hurrying, Kaa danced in front of the monkeys.

Baloo and Bagheera stood and could not move. Mowgli watched, and did not understand.

'*Bandar-log*,' said the deep voice of Kaa at last. 'Can you move?'

'Without a word from you, Kaa, we cannot move.'

'Come nearer to me,' said Kaa.

The lines of monkeys came nearer, and Baloo and Bagheera walked forward, too.

'Nearer,' hissed Kaa, and they all moved forward again.

Mowgli put his hands on Baloo and Bagheera to get them away, and the two animals woke up.

'Keep your hand on me, Mowgli,' whispered Bagheera, 'or I will go back to Kaa, and walk into his mouth.'

'It's only old Kaa dancing,' said Mowgli. 'Let us go.' And the three of them went away into the jungle.

'A python's dance is dangerous to watch,' said Baloo, 'even for us. Kaa will have good hunting tonight.'

'And now, Mowgli,' said Bagheera angrily. 'Baloo and I have fought hard for you. The monkeys have bitten

22

'Nearer,' hissed Kaa.

us and pulled us and hit us. And all this, man-cub, was
because you played with the *Bandar-log*.'

'It is true,' said Mowgli sadly. 'I am a bad man-cub.'

'The Law of the Jungle says we must punish you,'
said Bagheera. Baloo was happy that Mowgli was safe

and with them again, but he could not speak against the Law.

'It is right to punish me,' said Mowgli. 'I did wrong.'

Bagheera hit him, very softly for a panther, but very heavily for a little boy. Mowgli did not cry.

'Now,' said Bagheera, 'jump on my back, Little Brother, and we will go home.'

'Jump on my back, Little Brother.'

One of the good things about Jungle Law is that, after you are punished, the matter is finished.

4

The fight at the rock

Mowgli always went to the meetings of the Wolf-Pack, and there he learnt something new one day. If he looked hard at any wolf, the wolf could not meet his eyes and looked away. Mowgli thought this was funny; he did not understand that he was different from the wolves.

All the Jungle-People were his friends – but not Shere Khan, of course. Mother Wolf told him that the tiger wanted to kill him. 'One day you must kill Shere Khan. If you don't kill him, he will kill you.' But Mowgli forgot. He was only a boy, not a wolf.

Shere Khan still came often to that part of the jungle. Akela was older now and not so strong, and Shere Khan made friends with some of the younger wolves. Akela could not stop them, and Shere Khan began to make trouble for Mowgli. 'I hear you can't look into the man-cub's eyes,' he said, laughing, to the young wolves. And the young wolves began to get angry.

Bagheera, who had eyes and ears everywhere, knew something of this and told Mowgli. Mowgli laughed, but Bagheera went on, 'Open your eyes, Little Brother. Remember that Akela is old and he will not always be the leader of the Pack. Shere Khan has taught the younger wolves that a man-cub has no place with them. And soon you will be a man, not a man-cub.'

'But the wolves are my brothers. Why will they want to send me away?'

'Look at me,' said Bagheera, and Mowgli looked at him hard between the eyes. The big black cat turned his head away quickly. 'That is why,' he said. 'Not even *I* can look in your eyes. That is why they want to kill you. You are clever. You are a man.'

'I did not know these things,' said Mowgli quietly.

'Now listen. The day will soon come when Akela cannot kill his deer in the hunt. Then at the next meeting of the Pack the younger wolves will be against Akela and against you. When that time comes, go to the men's houses in the village and take some of their Red Flower. That will be a stronger friend to you than I or Baloo.'

The Red Flower was fire. All animals are afraid of it and do not call it by its name. 'I will get some,' said Mowgli. 'I will go and get it now, and keep it ready,' and he ran through the jungle to the village.

On his way he heard the sounds of the Wolf-Pack hunting a big deer. 'Show us that you are strong, Akela,' came the voices of the young wolves. 'Kill it!'

Mowgli stopped and listened, and he could hear that Akela did not kill the deer. 'So the time has come already,' he thought, and hurried to the village. He watched and waited, and soon he saw a child who was carrying a fire-pot. Mowgli jumped up, took the pot from him, and quickly ran away, back to the jungle. All that day he kept his fire alive with leaves and pieces of wood.

In the evening Tabaqui came and told him that the wolves wanted him at the meeting. Mowgli laughed, and went. When he arrived, he saw that Akela was not

Mowgli jumped up and took the fire-pot from him.

in his special place, on top of the rock, but beside it. That meant that another wolf could try to take Akela's place. Shere Khan was there, too, with all the younger wolves around him. Mowgli sat down, with the fire-pot between his legs. Bagheera lay beside him.

Shere Khan began to speak and Mowgli jumped up.

'Free People, is Shere Khan your leader? Does a tiger belong in the Wolf-Pack?'

'There is no wolf on the rock,' began Shere Khan, but the other wolves said, 'Let Akela speak.'

Akela looked up, old and tired. 'Free People, I have been your leader for many years. In all that time no wolf

27

has died in the hunt. But this time I did not kill my deer. The Law of the Jungle says that you can kill me now, but the Law also says that you must come one by one.'

No one spoke. Akela was old, but nobody wanted to fight Akela alone.

Then Shere Khan spoke. 'Bah! This old wolf is not important. He will die soon. It is the man-cub who has lived too long. Give him to me.'

'A man! A man!' cried most of the younger wolves angrily. 'A man does not belong in the Wolf-Pack.'

'Mowgli is our brother,' said Akela. 'He has eaten

'This time I did not kill my deer,' said Akela.

28

our food. He has slept with us. He has done nothing wrong. Let him go to his own place.'

'He is a man,' cried Shere Khan and most of the wolves.

Mowgli stood up, the fire-pot in his hands. He was very angry, and very sad.

'You have said many times that I am a man. I was your brother, but I will not call you my brothers again. *I* will decide on my life or my death, not *you*. I am a man, and to show you, I have brought the Red Flower with me.'

He dropped the fire-pot on the ground and some of the fire fell out. The wolves were very afraid and moved back. Mowgli held a long piece of wood in the fire and the end began to burn brightly.

'You are the leader now,' said Bagheera softly. 'Help Akela. He was always your friend.'

'Good,' said Mowgli. He looked at the frightened wolves. 'I go from you to my people – the world of men. But first . . .' and Mowgli went to Shere Khan. 'This killer of cows wanted to kill me. This is what men do to killers of cows,' and he hit Shere Khan on the head with the burning stick. The tiger was very frightened.

'Go now,' said Mowgli to Shere Khan. 'The next time I come to this rock, it will be with your dead body. I tell you this also, my brothers, you will *not* kill Akela – because *I* do not want that. Akela is free to live.'

Mowgli hit Shere Khan on the head with his burning stick.

And Mowgli jumped at the young wolves with his burning stick and they all ran away. In the end there were only Akela, Bagheera, and a few older wolves left. Then something began to hurt Mowgli inside him and, for the first time in his life, tears ran down his face.

'What is it? What is it? Am I dying, Bagheera?'

'No, Little Brother. You are a man, and these are men's tears. But you must go – the jungle is closed to you now.'

'Yes,' said Mowgli. 'I will go to men. But first I must say goodbye to my mother.' And he went to the cave and cried on Mother Wolf's coat.

'You will not forget me?' Mowgli said to his wolf-family.

'Never,' said his wolf-brothers. 'Come to the foot of the hill when you are a man, and we will talk with you.'

'Come soon, little frog,' said Father Wolf, 'because your Mother and I are getting old.'

'I will surely come,' said Mowgli, 'and I will bring the coat of Shere Khan and put it on the Meeting Rock.'

And in the morning Mowgli went down the hill alone to meet those strange things that are called men.

Tiger-Tiger

Mowgli knew that he had enemies now and he went far away. He ran until he came to a village in a place with many rocks and narrow valleys. Everywhere Mowgli could see cows and buffaloes. Some little boys were looking after the cows, but when they saw Mowgli, they shouted and ran away. Mowgli walked on until he came to the village.

He sat down by the gate. When a man came out of the village, Mowgli opened his mouth to show that he wanted food. The man ran back into the village and came back with a hundred other people. They all looked at Mowgli and saw the bite-marks on his arms and legs.

'Look,' said a man, 'those are the bite-marks of wolves. He is a wolf-child who has run away from the jungle.'

'He is a good-looking boy,' said one of the women. 'Messua, he looks like your little boy that was taken by the tiger.'

'Let me look,' said Messua. 'Yes, he is thin, but he looks like my son.'

'Take him to your house, Messua,' the villagers said. 'The jungle took your boy, and the jungle has given you this one back.'

The woman called Messua took Mowgli to her house and gave him milk and bread. This was Mowgli's first time in a house, and he did not like it. It felt like a prison.

'But I am a man now,' he thought, 'and I must do what men do. I must also learn to speak like men.' He knew all the many languages of the jungle, and so it was easy for him to learn the sounds of men. That first evening he learnt many words from Messua.

The boys shouted and ran away.

But that night he did not want to sleep inside the house. So he climbed out of the window, and went to sleep in a field near the village. Before he went to sleep, a soft grey nose touched his face. It was Grey Brother, the eldest of Mother Wolf's cubs.

'Wake, Little Brother,' he said. 'I bring news. Shere Khan has gone away. You burnt his coat with the Red Flower. But he says that, when he comes back, he will kill you.'

'I remember also what I said about Shere Khan,' said Mowgli. 'But it is good to have news. Will you always bring me news, Grey Brother?'

'Yes, Little Brother. But you will not forget that you are a wolf? You will not forget us when you are with men?'

'Never,' replied Mowgli. 'I will always remember that I love you all.'

For three months Mowgli learnt how to be like a man. He had to wear clothes, learn how to use money, and

In the evenings Mowgli sat with the villagers under a great tree.

34

how to work in the fields. In the evenings he sat with the villagers under a great tree, while the men told stories about the jungle and the animals. Once, when Buldeo, the village hunter, told a story about a tiger, Mowgli had to hide his face because he was laughing. At the end he said, 'Buldeo's stories are stupid. He knows nothing about the jungle.'

The villagers did not like this, and after that they sent Mowgli out every day with the other boys, to look after the herds of cows and buffaloes while they ate. Mowgli enjoyed this work, and usually went on alone, with a big group of cows and buffaloes.

One day he saw Grey Brother under a tree near the jungle. 'Shere Khan has come back, but he is hiding for a while. Then he is coming to kill you,' said Grey Brother.

'Very good,' said Mowgli. 'Tell me when he comes. Meet me at the river, by the big *dhak*-tree with golden flowers. I will watch for you there every day.'

Day after day Mowgli went out with the herds, but there was nobody at the *dhak*-tree. Then at last the day came when Grey Brother was waiting for him.

'Shere Khan has waited for a month, and is hoping that you have now forgotten about him,' said the wolf. 'He's going to wait for you at the village gate this evening. But now he is hiding in the big dry ravine of the Waingunga. I met Tabaqui this morning—' here

Grey Brother showed his teeth a little '—and before I broke his back, he told me all about Shere Khan's plan.'

'Has Shere Khan eaten today, or does he hunt empty?' The answer was life or death for Mowgli.

'He killed and ate this morning. And he has drunk, too.'

'How stupid he is!' said Mowgli. 'Does he think that I shall wait until he has slept?' He stood and thought for a while. 'The ravine of Waingunga! I can take the buffaloes round to the top end and chase Shere Khan down the ravine. After a meal, he cannot fight or climb easily. But I need a big group of cows at the bottom end of the ravine, to stop him escaping. Then we will catch him between the buffaloes and the cows. Can you help me, Grey Brother?'

'Not I alone,' said Grey Brother, 'but I have someone who will help me.' And the big grey head of Akela came out from the trees.

'Akela! Akela!' said Mowgli. 'I knew you would not forget me.' The two wolves ran here and there among the herd, and soon the cows and buffaloes were in two groups. Already, they were getting excited and dangerous. The other herd-boys, who were watching a long way away, ran back to the village with the news.

'Keep the cows together, Grey Brother,' called Mowgli. 'Drive them into the bottom end of the ravine

'Akela! Akela! I knew you would not forget me.'

and keep them there until we come down. Akela, you and I will take the buffaloes round to the top.'

They drove the buffaloes round in a big circle uphill. It took a long time because they did not want Shere Khan to hear them. At last Mowgli was ready. He stopped and shouted down the ravine.

'Shere Khan! It is I, Mowgli. It is time for our meeting!'

Mowgli rode on the back of Rama, the biggest of the buffaloes, and Akela chased the herd from behind. The buffaloes began to run down the ravine, faster and faster, and the ground shook under their heavy feet.

Shere Khan heard the noise and woke up. He knew what it was, and he began to run down the ravine. No tiger can hope to stand against a herd of buffaloes when they are moving fast. He looked for a way to escape,

The buffaloes ran down the ravine, faster and faster.

but the ravine was narrow, with high rocky walls. He had to go on, heavy with his dinner and his drink. Then he saw the cows at the bottom of the ravine, and turned. But it was too late. He fell under the feet of the buffaloes, and they ran over him like a river running down a mountain.

The buffaloes did not stop until they crashed into the herd of cows. Mowgli jumped off Rama's back and shouted to Akela and Grey Brother.

'It is done! Shere Khan is dead! He died the death of a dog, not a fighting tiger.'

Mowgli took his knife and started to cut the coat from Shere Khan's body. It was hard work. After an hour Mowgli was still working when suddenly he felt a hand on his back. It was Buldeo, the village hunter.

'Go and look after your buffaloes,' he cried angrily. '*I* will take this tiger's coat. I can sell it for a hundred rupees, and you can have one rupee for yourself.'

'No,' said Mowgli. 'I need this coat.'

'Listen, boy!' shouted Buldeo. '*I* am the village hunter, and I will take the coat, and keep all the money.'

Then Mowgli spoke to Akela in the wolf-language, and suddenly Buldeo was lying on his back on the ground with a big grey wolf standing over him.

'Buldeo,' said Mowgli, 'for a long time this tiger has wanted to kill me. But I have killed him.'

Buldeo was very afraid. Who *was* this boy, who could talk to wolves and kill tigers? 'Great King,' he said to Mowgli, 'I am an old man. I thought you were just a herd-boy. Let me go now, and I will go away.'

'Go, and peace go with you,' replied Mowgli, and he went on with his work.

It was nearly dark when at last he and the wolves pulled the great coat away from the tiger's body.

'Now we must hide this and take the cows and the buffaloes back to the village,' said Mowgli.

But when Mowgli came near the village, there was a crowd of people waiting for him at the gate. 'Go away, wolf-child!' they shouted. 'Go away, or we will kill you!'

Mowgli did not understand. Shere Khan – the tiger who killed cows and stole children – was dead, but people were angry with him. He turned away and looked up at the stars in the sky. 'No more sleeping in houses for me, Akela. Let us get Shere Khan's coat and go away.'

The moon climbed high in the sky, and the frightened villagers watched while Mowgli began to run across the fields, with the two grey wolves running at his side.

The moon was going down when Mowgli and the two wolves came to Mother Wolf's cave. 'The men do not want me, Mother,' called Mowgli. 'I have come home, and I have brought the coat of Shere Khan.'

Mother Wolf came out of the cave, very happy to see Mowgli again, and to know that Shere Khan was dead.

From the jungle came the deep voice of Bagheera. 'Little Brother, we are pleased to see you.'

Then Mowgli took the coat of Shere Khan and put it on the great rock at the wolves' meeting place. Akela lay on it and called, 'Look well, O Wolves!' And the Wolf-Pack came and looked, and saw that Shere Khan was dead.

'Now,' said Mowgli, 'I do not belong to the Wolf-Pack, or to the Man-Pack. I will hunt alone in the jungle.'

'And we will hunt with you,' said Grey Brother and the rest of Mother Wolf's cubs.

And Mowgli went away into the jungle and lived and hunted with his brothers, the wolves.

GLOSSARY

attack *(v)*   to try to hurt or kill someone

bite   to cut something with your teeth

chase   to run after someone or something

frightened   afraid

herd   a large group of cows (or other animals) that live and eat together

hiss   a long 'ssss' sound, which a snake makes

hunt *(v)*   to chase and kill animals for food

jungle   a thick forest in hot, wet countries

king   the most important man in a country

law   something that tells you what you must and must not do

leader   the person or animal that tells others what to do

look after   to keep someone or something well, and away from danger

master-word   a special or important word, that everybody knows

peace   a time when there is no fighting or trouble

punish   to hurt someone because he or she did something wrong

ravine   a long narrow place with high sides of rock

roar *(n)*   a long deep sound, made by animals like tigers

rupee   money used in India

sad   not happy

safe   not in danger

whisper *(v)*   to speak in a very low, soft voice

The Jungle Book

ACTIVITIES

Before Reading

1 **What do you know about jungles? Choose the best answers to these questions.**

1 What is the weather like in a jungle?
   a) It rains a lot.   d) It is very cold.
   b) It never rains.   e) It is very hot.
   c) It snows in winter.   f) It is warm, but not hot.

2 Which of these countries have jungles?
   a) Italy   d) Spain
   b) Brazil   e) India
   c) Canada   f) Japan

2 **Which of these things do you find in jungles? Underline the most usual things.**

beaches	elephants	rivers
birds	flowers	sheep
buses	fruit	shops
chickens	gardens	snakes
cinemas	hills	tigers
cows	monkeys	trees

3 Read the story introduction on the first page of the book, and the back cover. How much do you know now about the story?

Tick one of the boxes for each sentence. YES NO

1 The jungle is in Southern India. ☐ ☐
2 Mowgli is a wolf-cub. ☐ ☐
3 Mother Wolf wants to keep the baby. ☐ ☐
4 The baby is afraid of Mother Wolf. ☐ ☐
5 Mowgli dies while he is still a baby. ☐ ☐
6 A bear and a panther are his teachers. ☐ ☐
7 Shere Khan the tiger is Mowgli's friend. ☐ ☐
8 Mowgli grows up with his wolf family. ☐ ☐

4 What will happen in this story? Can you guess? Tick one of the boxes for each sentence.

 YES NO

1 When Mowgli grows up, some of the wolves want to kill him. ☐ ☐
2 Mowgli leaves the jungle and goes to live in a village. ☐ ☐
3 He goes to school and learns to read and write. ☐ ☐
4 Shere Khan the tiger goes away and forgets about Mowgli. ☐ ☐
5 Mowgli kills Shere Khan. ☐ ☐
6 Shere Khan kills Mowgli. ☐ ☐

45

While Reading

Read Chapter 1. Who said these words in the chapter?

1 'The man's cub belongs to us.'
2 'I will have this man-cub one day, you thieves!'
3 'I will call him Mowgli, the frog.'
4 'Let him run with the Pack. I myself will teach him.'
5 'It is bad to kill a man-cub.'
6 'Take him away, and teach him well.'

Read Chapter 2. Here are some untrue sentences about it. Change them into true sentences.

1 Mowgli always loved his lessons with Baloo.
2 The Monkey-People were quiet and clean.
3 The monkeys carried Mowgli away to a cave.
4 Baloo and Bagheera asked Chil the kite for help.
5 Bagheera called Kaa the python an 'old yellow fish'.
6 Mowgli wanted to stay with the Monkey-People.

Read Chapter 3. Choose the best question-word for these questions, and then answer them.

Who / What / Where / Why
1 . . . attacked the monkeys first?

2 . . . did Kaa the python go?

3 . . . did Mowgli hear in the dark room?

4 . . . did Mowgli tell Bagheera to get into the water?

5 . . . made a hole in the wall?

6 . . . did Kaa do in front of the monkeys?

7 . . . was Bagheera angry with Mowgli?

Read Chapter 4, and then complete these sentences with the best word.

1 The animals could not look into Mowgli's _____.

2 One day Akela could not kill his _____ in the hunt.

3 The wolves said that a man did not _____ in the Wolf-Pack.

4 Mowgli hit Shere Khan with a _____ stick.

5 Mowgli knew he had to go to the world of _____.

Before you read Chapter 5, can you guess what will happen? Tick one box for each sentence. YES NO

1 Mowgli forgets all about his wolf-family. ☐ ☐

2 He learns the language of men. ☐ ☐

3 He makes friends with other boys. ☐ ☐

4 He stays in the village for the rest of his life. ☐ ☐

5 Shere Khan makes a plan to kill Mowgli. ☐ ☐

6 The people of the village help Mowgli to kill
Shere Khan. ☐ ☐

47

After Reading

1 **Match the names with the animals in this story.**

Tabaqui	monkeys
Shere Khan	the leader of the Wolf-Pack
Baloo	a python
Bagheera	a kite
Akela	a jackal
Bandar-log	a wolf
Chil	a tiger
Kaa	a bear
Grey Brother	a panther

2 **Who do these sentences describe? Fill in the names.**

1 _____ teaches the Law of the Jungle to the wolf-cubs.

2 _____ is brown and yellow, and ten metres long. His dance is dangerous to watch.

3 _____ are noisy and dirty. They make many plans and forget them five minutes later.

4 _____ has green eyes and is as black as the night. He is clever, strong, and dangerous.

5 _____ kills cows and steals children. He is afraid of fire.

6 _____ eats anything, and makes a lot of trouble.

3 **How did Mowgli kill Shere Khan the tiger? Put these parts of sentences in the right order to make a paragraph of four sentences.**

1 They put the cows and the buffaloes into two groups

2 he made a plan

3 while Mowgli and Akela took the buffaloes to the top of the ravine.

4 One day Grey Brother came to tell Mowgli that

5 and then Grey Brother drove the cows into the bottom end of the ravine.

6 Shere Khan was hiding in the ravine of the Waingunga.

7 and asked Grey Brother and Akela to help him.

8 He kept the cows there

9 When Mowgli heard this,

4 **Now finish the story of the death of Shere Khan. Use the words below to complete the passage.**

because / so / so / when / and / and / but

_____ the buffaloes began to run down the ravine, Shere Khan heard the noise _____ woke up. He too began to run _____ he could not run fast _____ he was heavy with his dinner and his drink. The ravine was high and narrow _____ he could not climb out of it, _____ he could not get past the cows at the bottom. There was no way for him to escape, _____ he died under the feet of the buffaloes.

5 Here is a new illustration for the story. Find the best place
  in the story to put the picture, and answer these questions.

The picture goes on page _____
  1 Who are the characters in the picture?
  2 What did the man want to do?
  3 Why is he frightened?

Now write a caption for the illustration.

Caption: _____

6 In each of these groups of words from the story, one word does not belong. Which word is it, and can you explain why?

1 run, climb, swim, jump, think
2 cow, deer, kite, buffalo, jackal
3 sun, cloud, moon, cave, star
4 bite, hiss, whisper, roar, shout
5 hill, ravine, mountain, valley, garden
6 brother, hunter, father, sister, mother
7 angry, frightened, tired, tall, hungry

7 Many people have written stories about animals who can talk. Look at these ideas. Do you agree (A) or disagree (D) with them?

1 Animals can't talk.
2 Perhaps animals can talk, but humans don't understand their language.
3 Perhaps wolves can talk to wolves and monkeys to monkeys, but wolves can't talk to monkeys.
4 Animals can't speak like humans, but they use a language of things like sounds and smells.
5 Some animals are cleverer than humans.

8 Which animal did you like best in *The Jungle Book*? And which animal do you like best in real life? Explain why.

ABOUT THE AUTHOR

Joseph Rudyard Kipling was born in India in 1865. His parents, who were British, sent him to school in England when he was six, and he returned to India in 1882 to work as a journalist for an Indian newspaper. At that time India was part of the British Empire, and thousands of British people lived and worked there. Kipling wrote poetry and short stories about the life of these British people in India, and also about the way of life of the Indian people.

In 1889 Kipling, now famous because of his stories, came back to England. He married an American woman and for four years they lived in Vermont in the USA, where Kipling wrote *The Jungle Book* and *The Second Jungle Book*. Back in England, Kipling continued to write stories, novels, and poetry, and in 1907 he was the first English writer to receive the Nobel Prize for Literature. He died in 1936.

Today, Kipling's best-known novel is *Kim*, a story about a young Irishman and his adventures in India. He is also famous for his stories for children – the *Just So Stories* (with titles like 'The Elephant's Child' and 'The Cat that Walked by Himself') – and the two *Jungle Books*. There is a well-known Walt Disney film of *The Jungle Book*, made in 1967. The film has many fine songs, but is very different from Kipling's story of Mowgli's life and adventures in the jungle.

OXFORD BOOKWORMS LIBRARY

Classics • Crime & Mystery • Factfiles • Fantasy & Horror
Human Interest • Playscripts • Thriller & Adventure
True Stories • World Stories

The OXFORD BOOKWORMS LIBRARY provides enjoyable reading in English, with a wide range of classic and modern fiction, non-fiction, and plays. It includes original and adapted texts in seven carefully graded language stages, which take learners from beginner to advanced level. An overview is given on the next pages.

All Stage 1 titles are available as audio recordings, as well as over eighty other titles from Starter to Stage 6. All Starters and many titles at Stages 1 to 4 are specially recommended for younger learners. Every Bookworm is illustrated, and Starters and Factfiles have full-colour illustrations.

The OXFORD BOOKWORMS LIBRARY also offers extensive support. Each book contains an introduction to the story, notes about the author, a glossary, and activities. Additional resources include tests and worksheets, and answers for these and for the activities in the books. There is advice on running a class library, using audio recordings, and the many ways of using Oxford Bookworms in reading programmes. Resource materials are available on the website <www.oup.com/bookworms>.

The *Oxford Bookworms Collection* is a series for advanced learners. It consists of volumes of short stories by well-known authors, both classic and modern. Texts are not abridged or adapted in any way, but carefully selected to be accessible to the advanced student.

You can find details and a full list of titles in the *Oxford Bookworms Library Catalogue* and *Oxford English Language Teaching Catalogues*, and on the website <www.oup.com/bookworms>.

THE OXFORD BOOKWORMS LIBRARY
GRADING AND SAMPLE EXTRACTS

STARTER • 250 HEADWORDS

present simple – present continuous – imperative –
can/cannot, must – *going to* (future) – simple gerunds …

Her phone is ringing – but where is it?

Sally gets out of bed and looks in her bag. No phone. She looks under the bed. No phone. Then she looks behind the door. There is her phone. Sally picks up her phone and answers it. *Sally's Phone*

STAGE 1 • 400 HEADWORDS

… past simple – coordination with *and, but, or* –
subordination with *before, after, when, because, so* …

I knew him in Persia. He was a famous builder and I worked with him there. For a time I was his friend, but not for long. When he came to Paris, I came after him – I wanted to watch him. He was a very clever, very dangerous man. *The Phantom of the Opera*

STAGE 2 • 700 HEADWORDS

… present perfect – *will* (future) – *(don't) have to, must not, could* –
comparison of adjectives – simple *if* clauses – past continuous –
tag questions – *ask/tell* + infinitive …

While I was writing these words in my diary, I decided what to do. I must try to escape. I shall try to get down the wall outside. The window is high above the ground, but I have to try. I shall take some of the gold with me – if I escape, perhaps it will be helpful later. *Dracula*

... should, may – present perfect continuous – *used to* – past perfect –
causative – relative clauses – indirect statements ...

Of course, it was most important that no one should see
Colin, Mary, or Dickon entering the secret garden. So Colin
gave orders to the gardeners that they must all keep away
from that part of the garden in future. *The Secret Garden*

STAGE 4 • 1400 HEADWORDS

... past perfect continuous – passive (simple forms) –
would conditional clauses – indirect questions –
relatives with *where/when* – gerunds after prepositions/phrases ...

I was glad. Now Hyde could not show his face to the world
again. If he did, every honest man in London would be proud
to report him to the police. *Dr Jekyll and Mr Hyde*

STAGE 5 • 1800 HEADWORDS

... future continuous – future perfect –
passive (modals, continuous forms) –
would have conditional clauses – modals + perfect infinitive ...

If he had spoken Estella's name, I would have hit him. I was so
angry with him, and so depressed about my future, that I could
not eat the breakfast. Instead I went straight to the old house.
Great Expectations

STAGE 6 • 2500 HEADWORDS

... passive (infinitives, gerunds) – advanced modal meanings –
clauses of concession, condition

When I stepped up to the piano, I was confident. It was as if I
knew that the prodigy side of me really did exist. And when I
started to play, I was so caught up in how lovely I looked that
I didn't worry how I would sound. *The Joy Luck Club*

Alice's Adventures in Wonderland

LEWIS CARROLL

Retold by Jennifer Bassett

There, on top of the mushroom, was a large caterpillar, smoking a pipe. After a while the Caterpillar took the pipe out of its mouth and said to Alice in a slow, sleepy voice, 'Who are *you?*'

What strange things happen when Alice falls down the rabbit-hole and into Wonderland! She has conversations with the Caterpillar and the Cheshire Cat, goes to the Mad Hatter's tea party, plays croquet with the King and Queen of Hearts . . .

A Stranger at Green Knowe

LUCY M. BOSTON

Retold by Diane Mowat

When Ping sees Hanno in the zoo, he is excited, but also unhappy. Hanno is a magnificent African gorilla, big and black and much stronger than a man. But how can this wonderful wild animal live in a cage, behind bars and locked doors?

Then Hanno escapes from the zoo. And a few days later his footprints are seen near Green Knowe, the old house deep in the English countryside where Ping is spending his holiday . . .